there's coffee in the pot

cammie dennis

to the little girl inside of me —

you were right, love is supposed to be easy

dear reader,

we make plans and we follow a path
that we believe will bring us happiness,
but somewhere along the way,
we find out that our plans mean very little
and the path was never as defined as we thought it might be
– *life was always going to throw us a few curveballs*

finding myself was never a part of my plan,
but losing myself wasn't a part of it, either

after writing my first book,
I wasn't sure that I would write another one,
but there was still so much left to say
– *there was still so much left to heal*

there's coffee in the pot is an ode
to the things you do
for the people you love,
but more than that,
it is an ode to the little girl that I lost along the way

the pieces of poetry in this book were written in coffee shops,
on long drives, in conversations with friends, and in beautifully
messy places that have pieces of me written all over them

it is a collection of my world
and I am here to let you see it all through my eyes
– a set of eyes that is excited about life,
a set of eyes that is determined to find her happiness

the harsh truth is that heartbreak is hard
and falling out of love is even harder,

but finding yourself along the way
is a journey that should never be taken for granted

I wrote this book for the younger version of me who always knew
that there was more to life than what she had seen,
and if I could go back and tell her one thing,
I'd tell her this:

always be true to who you are,
never be afraid to tell someone to fuck off,
and if you ever need anything, I'll be here to help guide you
– you deserve more than a watered-down version of love,
and you've always known that

I hope that the words in this book
open your heart
to the possibility that love still exists,
and maybe the best parts of it
exist within you

and so I'll leave you with this:

go out and find who you are
and what you love,
and never apologize for being everything
that you've always wanted to be
– this world will try to strip you of your innocence,
but it is the most beautiful thing about you

I hope that wherever you are in this world, you find the love that
you've always deserved *because you do deserve it*

from my heart to yours, with love
cammie

i'll see you in the next life

if I see you in the next life
we can get drunk
and tell stories
about what could have been
if we had made it
in this one

this life
wouldn't have been mine
without you in it

in my dreams
I'm still laughing at your jokes
and you're still kissing me
in the back seat of the taxi

– how did we get this far from home
with no way back to each other?

sunday 4:07 pm

hey
I know it's been a while since we've talked,
I was just calling to say that I miss you
and I'm sorry I never told you this...

but I think I'm still in love with you –

end of message

somewhere between all of our fights
and me calling you on a payphone, *drunk*
we became strangers
who forgot that there was a time
when we shared sips of coffee
out of the cracked mug
that I bought for you on your birthday

maybe one day we'll get drunk
and tell each other
all of the secrets
we wish we had said back then,
or maybe we'll smile at each other
and laugh about what could have been,
but until that day
I hope you find someone to take my place

— *I hope she loves you better than I ever could*

I knew it was over
when your name in my phone
turned into numbers
and the last time I asked someone about you
was the last time I'd ask someone about you
and every last photo of us
has dissipated into the flames
of the fire
that my dad made
to keep us alive,
but missing you doesn't feel as heavy
at this time of night
and I'm sorry that it had to come out this way,

but I knew it was ending
before it was over

and now that it's over
the secret is out
– a love like ours was never going to last

was I good to you?

tell me that
or tell me anything at all

– I know we can't look each other in the face these days,
but was I good to you?

if I saw you across a crowded bar
and somehow,
someway,
we made it into each other's space
I would politely smile at you
and tell you that you've been missed,
but the whole time
I'd be wishing I could've told you
that out of all the people I've ever loved,
you were my most favorite

you saw a pretty face
and hips that curve
and you thought
that if you could trace
the outline of my body
with promises of forever
you would finally know
what it felt like
to be set free
from all of your sins
that have nothing to do with me

– I wish I had known that you were going to hurt me

I showed you what it means
to be loved,
unconditionally;
you showed me
that I needed to learn
how to love myself,
unconditionally

I knew we were never playing the same game
– I wanted you to change my last name,
but you wanted me to stay the same

I was always going to grow my own garden

I went to the coffee shop we used to go to

I ordered your favorite drink
and sat at our spot,
I stared out the same window
that watched us fall in love
– cars passed
and people talked
and I could still smell the same nostalgic scent
of coffee beans roasting,
but as soon as my lips touched the mug
I knew I couldn't be here anymore

– it doesn't taste the same without you

healing was never supposed to be linear

– I was always going to end up
on my kitchen floor
crying about you
two years later

no one ever told me
that it'd hurt this much
to fall out of love

you knew I'd ruin myself for you
and you let me

— that is not love,
that is not love,
that is not love

I wanted him to care the way that I do,
but you can't love someone into loving you

and you can't make people care
when they don't want to

I screamed at the top of my lungs,
"I fucking love you!"

he whispered back,
"I don't even know what love means."

I will never be the girl that I was before you

– pieces of her will exist,
but only ever in your memory

the way that I loved him
was not romantic
like you see in the movies,

it was romantic
like you see in a cemetery

I was always hoping it would come back to life

I met someone new

he doesn't kiss me like you do
and I can tell

I hope that when you see me next
you don't recognize the girl standing in front of you

– I hope you recognize that you're responsible
for the death of her innocence

I loved him
like a child
loves their favorite stuffed animal

– I never wanted to let go

sometimes you have to love people from afar
and let that be enough

– sometimes you have to let people go,
even when you aren't ready to give up

I didn't walk away because I stopped loving you,
I walked away because I learned how to start loving me

— it is not selfish to give yourself the love
that they never could,
it is not selfish to walk away
when it is no longer good

my best friend reminded me that,
"we accept the love we think we deserve"

– *I'm sorry you felt like you deserved a love that would never last,*

I tell myself as I walk away from the only love
that I ever thought would last

even after all of the times
I've been burned,
I still have so much hope
that I will find the kind of love
that doesn't hurt

– it took strength to stay this soft

you are a dirty weed
and I am a garden full of love

– it is no wonder that your love
could not fill me up

the world is angry
that I have opened up about my sadness

– they no longer have an excuse for treating me like
I'm the one who created all of the madness

"someone not wanting you
should be the beginning
of you wanting yourself"

I remind myself as I walk away
from yet another failed stage of love

I never knew love as a child

I only knew about passion
and madness,
but never love

– not even my room was my own

I can finally see
that losing you was never a loss

it was an open invitation
for me to finally come home
to the love of my own heart

– *this is me saying thank you*

I haven't been the same since you left

you broke me
and I swallowed all of the broken pieces
whole
so that you wouldn't step on them
and hurt yourself, too

– how does it feel to know that you broke the only person who ever really knew you?

you broke me so bad
that lonely began to take on a whole new meaning

I hope that even after all of the pain you've endured, you still find the strength to stand back up and face what hurts. I hope that somewhere along the way, you realize that the light at the end of the tunnel was always you – you were the only one who could ever save yourself. I hope you find the strength to wipe the tears dry and keep going. *You have to keep going.* The light you've been waiting for has always been waiting for you – all you had to do was realize that it was inside of you. You have to reignite the flame and let it burn down what no longer serves you. You have to keep going – *it will all be worth it in the end.*

I'll tell my new lover stories from that summer
but I won't tell him your name

I'll tell him about the night
that we fell into each other's arms
in the middle of a crowded bar
and you carried me home
because I didn't know
how to stand up on my own
but I won't tell him your name

I'll tell him about how you looked at me
in the back seat of the taxi
and kissed all of the scars
that your best friend left all over me
but I won't tell him your name

I'll tell him about how you saved me
when I didn't know I needed it
because you loving me
was something I didn't know I needed

but I won't ever tell him your name

– I'll never let him hate you
in the ways that I always wanted to
so I won't tell him your name

even the worst things I have done
were done out of love

– could you say the same?

I hope that somewhere down the road
we cross paths at the local coffee shop
or the corner store
that used to sell your favorite bottle of wine

I hope that our eyes meet
and you can see all of the stories
that you never got to be a part of

I hope that you have it in you
to smile at me
and remember me as the girl
that once knew you

I hope that even then
you know that my love for you
was unlike anything you ever knew

I hope that we smile at each other
like real lovers do
and you're reminded
of the girl you thought you knew

– loving you was sweet,

but forgetting you is what finally set me free

in the dark of night,
I lost the safest home
that I had ever known

– in the light of day,
I was forced
to build my own

everything screams before it dies

and tonight
I'm drowning in the silence
of forgetting you

daisies & roses

I know he loved me,
at least I'd like to think he did,
but the difference between me and him
is that my love was made
from daisies and roses
and all he could ever give me
were bullet holes and broken promises

I always thought
it was the kind of love
that could save me,
but it turns out
it was the only one
that knew how to break me

kissing him was like tasting poison
and liking it

fragile love

if love is handed to me
in a fragile glass box
there is no doubt
that it will break when it drops

but if love is handed to me
in layers of titanium and steel,
or anything to keep it locked and sealed,
then there is no chance in hell
that it could ever break

– I don't want your fragile love

if someone cares about their standing in your life,
then they will do something about it

– you should never have to convince someone to love you

I still whisper secrets about you
to the moon,

she's the only one who ever knew
how much I loved you

I have few words
left inside my body
that are still blushed
by your existence,
but as I put the swords down
and call a truce
I need you to know
that it took every last piece of me
to walk away from you

– in every other universe,
I would've married you

shades of you

without judgment,
without apprehension,
I took off the glasses
that had been blinding me
for a lifetime

– the roses
could no longer
color my glasses
with gentle hues of red,

now I only see through
vibrant shades of truth

you never knew how much I loved you,
but loving you was the only thing I knew how to do

we had melodies of love
dancing between us
like kerosene in a fire

– I forgot that every song
must end at some point,

I forgot that every fire
must burn out eventually

even after all this time,
I still check up on you

– you look happy,

I hope it's true

"no contact"

you can still call me
if you ever need me
– even though we said
we wouldn't talk anymore,
it doesn't mean
that I care any less
than I did before

– you will always have a seat at my table

the hardest part about letting go of a version of yourself that you once knew is recognizing that if you don't let go, you'll be stuck in the same place until you do. it's grieving the loss and then setting it free. it's reminding yourself that what's meant for you will always be. you have to remember that letting go of who you once were is the hardest thing you will do in this life – but you have to remember that in order to refill your cup with something new, you have to let go of the version of yourself that you once knew. *and your cup will be filled with something new, but you have to be willing to let go of what no longer serves the new version of you.* you have to guide yourself to where you want to be. you have to offer this version of yourself compassion and kindness for all that she's been through. you have to tell the old version of yourself, "I'll take care of us like no one else knew how to – *you will always be safe with me.*"

don't ever let someone who is not ready to love you
make you feel like you are unlovable

– don't ever let someone else's inconsistencies with themselves
make you question the worth of yourself

I miss the days
when the cages around my heart
weren't suffocating me

– I miss who I was before you hurt me

loving him was like having a three-day hangover,

except I haven't had a drink since last week

I was falling in love
while you were pulling us apart

– our story was over
before it even had the chance to start

we always had an expiration date

I got lost in the rabbit hole of realities
that I created in my head
about what you and I
could have been

– maybe you wrote forever on my arm,
but it was only ever in my head

I cry every last tear I have
inside this cold and aching body
and I scream out for you to tell me
that you loved me
as much as I loved you
but I won't reach back out
to tell you that I still love you

this time around,
I'll put on my mascara
and I'll dance around my room
and I'll learn how to love myself
better than you ever knew how to

second third or hundredth chances

I have it in me to forgive
but I don't think I'll ever forget

– our chances have run out,
just like you did

I kept my hands clean
and my words flirty

you threw punches
and kept your knuckles stained bloody

– when are you going to learn that hating me
was never going to make you love yourself any better?

the worst part about missing you
was that I didn't know if I was allowed to

– you were never really mine,

is it okay if I cry?

even in another lifetime
I'd recognize you
with my eyes closed

I've always known you by heart

if you ever find yourself on this side of town
don't ever hesitate to call
– even with nobody by your side
and all odds stacked against you
I'll always be someone you can run home to

and if there ever comes a day
that the dial tone
is the only thing you can reach
– call out for me

I would know your scream
from a thousand miles away

"it wasn't all bad, was it?"

"no, it wasn't all bad."

"we laughed a whole lot, didn't we?"

"yeah, we were always laughing."

some days
I go back to the place
where we first met
and I replay the memories
to remind myself
that it wasn't all in my head

– *you were there, too*

take the time to get to know yourself. write words that only make sense to you. find freedom in solitude. make friends with the person in the mirror. make your bed. make some coffee. turn up the radio and let go of the things that make you feel like less than your best. keep moving – and take it all one day at a time. remember that it is okay to choose yourself. it is not your responsibility to carry everyone else's burdens when your hands are full of your own. it is okay to say no. empty out the old and make room for the new – it is not selfish to fill up your cup with things that make you feel free. you deserve to feel peace, you deserve to feel happy – and more than anything, you deserve to feel loved. you have always been good enough –it's time that you start to believe it.

I cried about you in the car today
and then I went to the grocery store
to pick up milk

– I don't know if I'd call that strength,
but it's the only word I know how to use
when I talk about letting go
of the only person I ever really knew

did I ever really know you?

closure comes at the most unexpected times
and in the most unexpected ways

– one day you wake up
and you realize
that you haven't thought about them
in three days

the songs that used to make you cry
now make you want to dance

the idea of seeing them out
doesn't hold as much weight

the stories that mention their name
don't make you want to scream out about the pain

closure comes quietly
and without hesitation

it's like watching the seasons change
– one day it's winter
and the sun is setting at 5 pm
and the clouds cover the dimly lit sky,
but the next day you wake up
and the birds are chirping
and the sun is shining
and it's almost summer again

it's finally summer again

it rained today
in the middle of July

– I forgot that even the world weeps
for who we used to be

the eulogy of who she used to be

I knew I couldn't love her
in the ways that she needed me to,
but I would've set myself on fire
or drowned my heart in bottles of whiskey
if it meant that she would come back here
and kiss me,
one last time

I miss the girl that I used to know

I watched honey spill from her lips
as she tried to tell me
that she still loves me,
but after years of tasting poison,
the idea of tasting something *so sweet*
didn't sit right with me

– she was always too good
for someone like me

if you have the strength to let go
of the people who no longer serve you,
give yourself some extra love today

– it is no easy feat saying goodbye to someone who is still alive

I can't change how it ended

but I can begin to heal
the way that it hurt me

as I started walking toward the life
that I've always wanted to live
I stopped for a moment
to look back at who I've been

– I smiled at her
and she smiled back,

"keep going, love — the world has been waiting for you,
and we will be okay without you."

she's a glimmer of hope
in a world full of darkness

she's a shining light
among a million dead light bulbs

anyone who has felt the warmth radiate
from the soft side of her heart
knows that if you were lucky enough
to meet this part of her,
you were lucky enough
to be held
by more than just her arms

she undressed herself when she spoke her mind

everyone watched
as she peeled off each layer
as if it were an art exhibit
dedicated to her thoughts

she carried her pain beautifully

– it was as if no one had ever laid a hand on her,
but the truth was

the whole world had

some people go to church to feel holy

I stare into her eyes
and it's like bathing in sunlight

strings attached

I saw her dancing in the middle of the street
and I knew that nothing was going to stop me
from falling in love with the girl
who attached every part of her
to every part of me

she was effortlessly cool

like something you see
in the movies

she knew more about love
than love knew about itself

a sad soul
with heavy blue eyes
and sunflowers growing out of her mind

– *her*

and when she speaks
we listen

and when she laughs
we dance

and when she cries
we all cry

she has an effect on this world
that is more than what meets the eye,

a soul like hers is hard to find

everything about her is one of a kind

"keep going," she said.
"you look beautiful when you care."

she was losing her mind
and finding herself all at once

– it was beautiful to watch a girl like her
take something broken and make it whole

if you ever get the chance to love her
love her fearlessly,
and love her kindly,
but whatever you do,
do not be reckless with her heart

it is made of gold
and even the smallest crack
could break her soul

lucky is the man
who gets to make her laugh
for the rest of his life

the most dangerous thing
about a girl like her,
is that even at her worst,
she loves herself entirely

– even at her lowest,
she'll smile at you
with tears in her eyes

she knew that the secret to life
was to be as passionate
and crazy as possible

– she knew that if she were to be herself,
entirely,
it would scare off the people
who did not see her love
as a priority

not everyone understood her,
but she didn't mind

– she didn't live to be understood,
she lived to be free

I remember the first time I heard her laugh

– I thought that the flowers were speaking to me

she is guarded,
but not by choice

– the world had made her that way

she was art
and dead roses
and things that didn't make sense
to anyone
but me

– she was the tortured type of pretty

in a world
that is so terrified to be itself
she stood out
as her own

– she made the moon look full
all year round

her kisses taste like sweet cherries
and all of the love I've never experienced

I hope you see it one day. I hope you see that you change people for the better. I hope you see yourself the way that everyone else does. I hope you see that your honesty creates integrity and that your laughter can brighten even the darkest rooms. I hope you see that even when you speak few words, people stop to listen. I hope you see that you are the guiding light in many people's lives. *You create a sense of safety. You create a sense of freedom for the soul*. You make people want to feel whole. You make them feel like they can be themselves without judgment. You make them want to be strong and kind and full of love. You make people see the good in everything. You change people's mind with the words that you write and you blossom like a flower in the dark. And even after all this time, I hope you finally see that you never had to change who you are to be loved – *all you ever had to do was accept that your soul is made of pure gold.* This world needs more people like you.

she poured love into everyone that she met
because she knew what it felt like to live with an empty soul

all of the terrible things in life
seem to dissipate
when she looks into my eyes

– it's as if the world stops for a moment
for me to be loved back to life

she doesn't need empty conversations
about sweet nothings

she needs a place
where she can lay all of her armor
and unravel all of the pieces of herself
that she has yet to let the world see

– *she needs someone who knows what real love means*

we cannot undo
what's already been done
but we can begin to heal it

– an open wound is far more volatile than a scar

to be lost
means there is still time
to be found

to be sensitive
is to be touched
by every little thing

– it is no wonder my body is riddled with scars

the only person who I owe an apology to is myself:

I'm sorry I didn't believe you when you told me
there was more to life than what we had seen,

I'm sorry that I convinced you
that love was not supposed to be easy

she knew how to heal her heart

but she didn't know how to unlove
all of the people who broke it

grieving the living

that's the thing about loving someone
– you don't get to decide when you miss them
after they're gone

you embracing yourself
in all of your messiness
and imperfectness
is what makes the people around you
want to be more of themselves

– no one ever expected you to be perfect

your effect on this world
is far greater than you could ever know

— people wait for the days
that they get to experience
someone like you

"no one's got you like I do,"

I whisper to my 10-year-old self

nothing compares to the way that girl smiles
when she's looking up at the moon

– they have a secret language that even I don't know

the pain I went through
was never poetic
or even beautiful,
it was blood-stained ruthlessness
and people who wanted me dead

— the old version of me died
so I guess you all win

we can go anywhere we want,
my dear,
but we cannot go back

– we will never be able to go back

"I have nothing to give you,"
I say with empty hands and a full heart.

"your time is the greatest gift you could ever give me,"
my mother reminds me.

I wish that I could go back in time
to when my father was young
so I could give him a hug
to remind him
that everything is going to be okay

– for today,
I will tell him that I love him
before he goes to work
and hope that is enough
to heal all of the hurt
that he felt
before I existed

"I wouldn't be me
without you,"
I remind him.

you have a big heart for a reason. you were put on this earth to spread love and be loved, but you also deserve to receive love. you have a sensitive soul and you feel everything so deeply, and after all of the times that you've given your love to everyone around you, it's time that it finds its way back to you. you were always meant to feel this much. you were always meant to give love, even when it was not given back to you. you were always meant to be a light in people's lives – now it's time for you to receive all of the love that you've given out over time. don't give up now – all of the love that you deserve is on its way back to you. you deserve the kind of love that people tell stories about. you are too full of love to give up.

even as a child
she knew that the world was not kind

– the world was always cruel to the most sensitive souls,

and a pure soul will always be misunderstood
by those who live through facades

walk, don't run

there is still time to be everything that you want to be. there is still time to grow, learn, and live. they say you must run towards what you want, but where's the fun in that? slow down the pace of your life. walk towards what you want. enjoy the things that you see. keep your eyes peeled for anything that breathes light into your life. water the flowers that will grow. bask in the sunlight that shines around you. stand still in the moment, and let it engulf you. let your life play out as it should – there is still so much time to get where you want to be. the universe is not in a rush, so why must you be?

you think you're hard to love,
but the truth is, you just haven't found your people yet.

you're the type of person who knows what you want and you're not willing to settle – and people know that. people see the way that you move through life with your heart on your sleeve and it scares them. your confidence speaks for itself. your love is the essence of your entire being. you are the type of person who is hard to find – you show up as the most authentic version of yourself, no matter who is around. you never shy away from an uncomfortable conversation, and you never let people tell you what to do. you find peace in solitude and you never give up on your dreams. *in a generation that plays a losing game – you've already won.*

our generation prides itself on the idea that the one who cares less is the one with the power in the relationship, but the truth is that love is not about power. love is about letting someone see you for everything that you are. be the one to care more. be the one to break the cycle. the truth is that you will meet many people in your life – some you meet for a reason, some you meet for a season, and some of them stay for a lifetime. and the thing about meeting the people who are meant to love you for a lifetime, is that they will love you effortlessly – for everything that you are. hold out for them – they've been waiting for you to love them back. *you are not hard to love – you just haven't met your people yet.*

it was never a question of whether or not she was worth it
– it was only a question of whether or not she knew it

it is all of the most ordinary things that make life worth living

it's spinning around in your bedroom to the song that used to make you cry. it's standing at the bar with your best friend waiting for a drink, laughing about the story you told her last week. it's smiling at a stranger and seeing them smile back. it's waking up to the sun peeking through your blinds on a Saturday morning, with a full day of plans waiting for you. it's sharing a glass of wine with all of your best friends and telling stories from the week – laughing at the good parts, holding hands through the hard parts, and enjoying every part because it's a Tuesday and you're sharing a glass of wine with the people that you love. it's hugging your father before you leave for the airport and telling your mother she looks beautiful while she gets ready. it's confiding in your siblings about something that hurts. it's sharing how you feel with someone you trust and letting them see a different side of you – a side that they will instantly love. it is all of the most ordinary things in life that are saturated with the most goodness.

life is not always easy, but if you have the right people by your side – people you can laugh with, people you can cry with, people who make you feel special, people that support you – then the world starts to feel a little bit less lonely. and it's the most ordinary things that become the stories worth telling.

you won't ever find the same love twice

– remember that when you try to reopen the door that you once closed

if you've come to find
the girl that you left behind,
the one with tears in her eyes
– you'll be looking for a lifetime

she isn't the same anymore
and the old her isn't coming back
to even out the score

she isn't who she used to be,
she became everything
that you said she couldn't be

she finally found her place in this world
without you by her side

she finally found the courage
to follow all of her wildest dreams

– so if you come back to find her
you'll finally see
that the girl you once knew
finally set herself free

I hope that you find the best parts of yourself this year. I hope that when the sun comes peeking through the clouds, your favorite parts of yourself do, too. I hope that you meet someone new – someone who changes you for the better. I hope that you enjoy every moment that you spend with the people that you love. I hope that you plant flowers in gardens and plant kisses on people's faces. I hope that you let yourself become all of the things you've always wanted to be. I hope that you give yourself the time and space to shine as bright as you know you can. I hope that you feel heard. I hope that you feel seen. And most of all, I hope that you feel loved. I hope that this year brings you back to your favorite parts of yourself.

if you can't find it outside of you
that means it is somewhere inside of you
waiting to be
seen,
heard,
recognized,
acknowledged
but most of all,
loved

even if you know why it happened,
it won't make it hurt any less

– this is your closure

she's a mystery to most,
but if you look a little closer,
she's an open book
waiting to be read
by the right person

– and not everyone knows
how to translate
the language
of a wild soul

that's the thing about girls like her
– her light shines bright
no matter who's around,
but the thing about a light that bright
is that it tends to shine
on the darkest parts
of everyone else

– she'll show you every part of yourself
whether you like it or not

she'll love every part of you
even if you cannot

girls like you deserve the world
and he could barely give you a piece of his own

– you deserve someone who knows your worth,

you deserve someone who can fill up your cup
more than halfway full

everything i've learned about love,
so far

send the text. say the thing that you want to say. fall in love and then get back up. tell people that you love them while you can. make messy art and write words across your bedroom wall. call your best friend who lives across the country. hug your mom. tell your dad that he did a good job. bring your sister flowers. fall in love, *again and again and again*. fall in love as many times as you can. be passionate and a little bit crazy, and let the right people find you. keep going. keep growing. keep loving. everything will fall into place, *exactly at the right time.*

I write about romantic love
as if it's the only thing I've ever known

but the truth is
that my best love,
my most favorite love,
is the one that I found inside myself

– and falling in love with who I am
has been anything but romantic

girls

conversations in bar bathrooms
holding hands through a crowd
an extra spritz of perfume before we leave
sharing different shades of blush
laughing till we cry
heavy pours of wine
"don't look now,
but he's coming toward us"
"I've got your back,
don't worry"
"I love you,
even with tear-stained cheeks
and blood on your back,"
it's all of us until the end

– thank you to the girls who exist in my world

thank you for watering my flowers
when I had nothing left to give

– to the friends that are like family

love is not about trying to change
and deconstruct people
into being a version of themselves
that you would be proud of,
love is about letting people grow
into the best versions of themselves
over many years
and many mistakes,
many good days
and just as many bad ones,
love is about being there to support their growth
and help them water their garden
when they can't water their own

– love is about letting people be who they are
and giving them the space to grow
while you also water your own

and on my search to find love
I found something much greater
than the kind of love that we chase

– *I found myself*

closure is not synonymous with forgiveness

closure means it's over,
forgiveness means taking back what was always yours

– compassion is the greatest gift you could give yourself

you keep everyone at a distance
as if that's going to make them love you
in the way that you always needed them to

– who told you that you don't deserve to be loved
exactly as you are?

dear best friend,

thank you for showing me what real love looks like

– I wouldn't be the same me, without you

on being present in life:

it was always this beautiful,
I was just looking at everything else

I had red wine
dripping from my lips
on a crisp Friday night
in the middle of February
and even though you told me
you hate the taste of sour grapes
you still kissed me
like I meant something to you

– is this what real love does for you?

when I met him
we compared the blood stains
on our backs
and all of the scars
across our hearts
and we slowly fell in love
with picking up the mess
that our past lover's
left for us to clean

I'm dancing around the kitchen
and he's kissing me
and the whole world is watching us
fall in love
over a bottle of wine

kissing him was like writing poetry
with our tongues
across the walls of each other's cheeks

meeting you was like walking into a house
that I had never been to
and instantly knowing that I was home

I hope that when he runs his hands across my heart
he can feel the warmth of a new start

– I hope he doesn't find the scars
that someone else imprinted across my body

I'm building a home for myself
where doors don't slam
and people don't yell
and love is scattered across a kitchen table
that was built with kindness and respect,
I'm building a home for myself
where the floors can be painted yellow
and the tables can be painted blue
because there is no right way to do anything
except to do it with you,
I'm building a home for myself
that will echo the feelings
that live deep inside my chest
and you will know that
when you step into the rooms
that were built by people
who love one another
with nothing but respect,
I'm building a home for myself
that was made for lovers like me
where there is space for you to be
everything that you've always wanted to be

to the boy who healed my heart:

I hope you know how you've inspired me
to be the person
who I've always wanted to be

– I hope you know that you put life back into me

real love isn't going to startle you
out of a peaceful slumber
and ask you to change who you are,
real love is going to walk in
with quiet feet
and whisper feelings of hope
that bring each other peace,
real love is going to walk towards you
with arms open wide
and love that comes free
and gently climb into a bed
that was built for lovers
who know what it means

– real love is more than skin-deep

meeting you
reminded me
that there is still so much love
yet to be found

soulmates

in our last lifetime,
I found you
and you found me
and we helped each other breathe

– in this one,
I get to hear you sing
as we drive along
listening to our favorite songs

I think that the purpose of life
is to love everything we have
while we still have it

– we won't always have it

we must love it all
while we can

to me,
you are exceptional

– I'm sorry that no one has told you this yet

healing with someone you love:

I can hold your hand while you do it,
but I can't do it for you

I put too much creamer in my coffee
and I add too much honey to my tea
so when I say that I love you
this is what I mean:

I will give you everything that I have
and then some more
because when I fall in love
I'll always be the one to say
that I love you more

– real love doesn't keep score

maybe beautiful things do get second chances

– I know this because I gave myself another chance
to live the life that I've always wanted to live

meeting you was on accident,

loving you was on purpose

meeting you reminded me that true love still exists
and maybe I'm not alone in all of this

– this world seemed so small before I met you

if forever had a face
it would be the same one you gave me
the night you told me
you could easily fall in love
with someone like me

you remind me of all the things
I've ever loved since childhood

"find what you love and let it kill you"

– no,
find what you love
and let it love you

unconditional love

I don't care how bad it's been

– even at your worst,
you are still my most favorite

the saying goes,
"till death do us part,"
but even I know
that death could not keep
our souls apart
so I am here to say
that whether it's this lifetime
or the next
my heart will always find you

– you will always have a home
as long as I am here

when you tell me that you love me
please don't use the word 'pretty'
or outline the spaces of my body,
tell me that my eyes are full of words
that you cannot wait to read,
tell me that every time I walk into a room
you feel at home,
tell me that the words I speak
are dripping from my mouth with honey,
tell me that my mind is a maze
that you will spend your whole life
learning to navigate,
tell me that you love me
but only define me by my intelligence,
tell me that my ability to love
is like nothing you've ever experienced,
tell me that the way I move through the world
is like watching the way that flowers bloom,
tell me that you love me
but not because of my body

– tell me that my imperfections
are the things you love most about me

love is a funny thing

I knew a boy for 10 years, and it took him breaking my heart
for me to finally accept that I had fallen deeply in love with him

I knew you for 2 days, and it took one look in your eyes
to know that you were going to change my mind about love
for the rest of my life

– you reignited hope into a cold, dying heart

the greatest tragedy I have ever known
was loving people
who did not want to grow

– *we cannot water the weeds*

the little things

laying in bed after a long day. belting out lyrics in the car with your best friend. opening the windows at dusk. sunsets in November. laughing until you cry. dancing in the kitchen to Lovers Rock. the moment before you kiss someone for the first time. linking arms with your friends as you walk through a crowded bar. talking to your mom about your favorite things. laughing with your siblings when you finally get to see them again. holding hands with your friends. the feeling you get when someone rests their head on your shoulder. the first cry after a long period of feeling nothing. smiling at someone from across the room because your eyes speak words you cannot say out loud. the first beach day of summer. listening to someone talk about something that they love. being in love. smiling at strangers. strangers smiling at you. making your favorite meal on a Sunday night. letting someone love you for exactly who you are. making room for someone at a crowded table. taking the long way home so you can listen to your favorite song. unexpected text messages. your favorite person being in the same room as you. feeling understood by someone. the look someone gives you when they know that they're falling in love with you. feeling heard. feeling seen. feeling loved. feeling your feelings.

love is when you wake up early to make yourself coffee before you go to work. love is waiting for someone while they tie their shoe. love is holding someone's hand when they need it most. love is letting someone be free to be whoever they want to be. love is simple and love is kind, and even though I don't know everything about love, *I know that it shouldn't make you cry.*

ways to say I love you

call me when you get home
I saw this and thought of you
have you eaten today?
did you get home safe?
I got extra for you
this song reminded me of you
how do you feel today?
tell me all about it
dance with me
you look beautiful
you make me feel seen
I told my mom about you
my dad's going to love you
seeing you is my favorite part of the day
knowing you has been my greatest gift
I couldn't imagine life without you
you make me feel safe
"it's a long story..." "I have time"
– I love you

I don't feel loved
when I have to pretend
to be someone I'm not
– I feel loved when I get to dance
in front of an open window
in the middle of January,
I feel loved when I can cry at 2 PM
about something that I haven't thought about in three years,
I feel loved when I get to be unique and authentic
and as ordinary as can be,
I feel loved when I get to say what's on my mind
without having to think twice,
I feel loved when I'm not thinking about
who I have to be
and I get to be who I want to be

– I feel most loved when I get to show up as the rawest version of me

"you are the same version of yourself,
no matter who you are around"

– a compliment that I will never forget,
from a person that I will always love

you tell me that you're hard to love
but then you go and plant flowers in my mind
and kiss me where it hurts
and I wonder who it was
that told you
you are hard to love

– loving you is the easiest thing
that I have ever done

make the most of what you have right now. be vulnerable and be kind, even to those who do not want to accept it. tell people you love them. tell people what they mean to you. walk through life without blinders on. be so full of love that no one, not even the devil, could knock you down. be so full of life that the trees begin to sing when you step outside. be the person that you always knew you could be – the one who doesn't give a fuck what anyone thinks. be cool and be kind and be whatever you want to be – the world has been waiting for you to set yourself free.

I want dinner parties
with belly laughs
and conversations about the universe
I want overflowing glasses of wine
with a side of sarcasm and wit
I want love
spread across a table
that was set by people
who know what it's like
to grieve versions of themselves
that no longer exist
I want a warm bed
with a lover
that knows how to love me right
– I want more than what I've had
and I know that's not too much to ask

everything I've learned about love

the new cliche says, "everything I've learned about love, I've learned from the women in my life," but I didn't know the truth about this until it was time. I didn't know the truth about this until I watched my sister wipe my tears dry after I drank one too many glasses of wine because the boy I once loved was someone that I could no longer recognize. I didn't know the truth about this until my best friend gripped my hand as we walked into the bar and she could see the look on my face as I smiled at the person who left me with all of these scars. I didn't know the truth about this until I was held hostage in my friend's apartment because 3 am had a funny way of making me believe that maybe he meant it when he said he still wanted me, but she knew better than to watch me leave. I didn't know the truth about this until every last word about him spilled out of my mouth for the hundredth time in a row, and even then, she didn't hang up the phone. I didn't know the truth about this until I finally let myself see that all of the love I was looking for was already staring back at me — but this time, it wasn't dressed up in trucker hats and baggy board shorts; it was dancing on tables in dresses that men call "too short", it was laughing until I cried and then letting her wipe my new mascara dry, it was cheek kisses as we said hello, no one walking out the door and hearing someone say "tell them more". it was always more beautiful than I ever thought it could be – it was the kind of love that helped set me free.

home

I can't wait to dance on tables with you
and kiss under the moonlight
for everyone to see,
I can't wait to smile from across the room
and know that someone who loves me
is looking back at me,
I can't wait to eat pizza on the floor
and stain your favorite shirt blue
with all of the love that I have for you,
I can't wait to look into your eyes
and know that even with someone else in my space
there is nothing left to hide,
I can't wait for you to see every part of me
and have you whisper back
that you can't believe you found me,
I can't wait to know about what your sister did to you
when you were three
and run my fingers across all of the scars
that you never let anyone see,
I can't wait to hear all of your stories
and listen to all of your woes,
but most importantly,
I can't wait to know
that we finally made it home

– *home for me is wherever you are*

even the bad days
are still filled
with so much love

3 am conversations
are made for
confessions of love
and letting someone see you
in your most vulnerable state

how to know you're successful:

you woke up today

you have hopes and dreams – even if they seem far out of reach

you have people who love you and want to know how you're doing

you know who you are – even if it's only a small piece of who you desire to be

you can smile and laugh and cry and let yourself be human

you are kind to others

you hold space for your pain and your joy

you have a hand to hold – even if it's your own

you exist in a world that is set on breaking you, yet you still stand out as the bright light that you know you can be

– the fact that you are still here
is reason enough to be proud of yourself,

your success speaks for itself

tell her about it

tell her that when she smiles at you
the whole world stops for a moment,
tell her that when she laughs
there's a piece of you that heals
from her happiness,
tell her that she looks beautiful
even when she's wrapped up in a three-day-old outfit,
tell her about the way your heart stopped
the first time you met her,
tell her about the moment
when you knew you were going to marry her,
tell her everything you could ever think of
and don't leave a single detail to the imagination

tell her about the way that you've waited
your whole life
to meet someone like her

tell her that all of the heartbreaks
and all of the hardships
were all worth it
because it led you to her

tell her that you love her
and never let her go,
tell her that everything about her
makes you want to grow
into the best version of you

tell her that this life wouldn't be yours,
without her in it

to my next love:

I'm out in the garden
tending to my own needs

p.s. I left coffee in the pot for you

the more I learn to love myself
the more I recognize all of the ways
that other people could not love me

– it wasn't my fault that they couldn't love me
in the ways I needed them to,

it's wasn't their fault that they couldn't love
in the ways I wanted them to

there is love in listening. listening to your best friend cry at 3 am. listening to the story that your mom is telling you about her first heartbreak. listening to the thoughts in your head that remind you that you are worthy. listening to the music play in an almost empty bar at closing time. listening to the advice you hear from the old lady you met at the local coffee shop. listening to the birds chirp outside your window on a cool summer day. there is love in listening to everything people have to say – listening is a safe space. it's all full of so much love.

– *it's always been about love*

where I find love

skinny dipping in the ocean at 3 am
laughing with my best friend in the bar bathroom
shared kisses with strangers who will become lovers
dancing in the middle of busy streets
laying in the sun with music playing
telling stories in the kitchen
finding a new song that I will listen to on repeat
shared glances across crowded rooms
secrets shared in the middle of big parties
telling someone how I feel about them,
despite what their reaction might be
small gestures from strangers
hearing someone tell me about their family
journaling about the things that hurt
allowing myself to be in the present moment

love letters to myself:

your refusal to give up is what makes you strong
– not the things that you've been through
or the things you've cried about in your room,
I tell myself

– knocked down nine times, get up ten,
I tell myself

that's resilience,
I tell myself

I'm so proud of you for still dreaming
and holding out hope
that the things you love will come to life,
I tell myself

you are the blueprint of love
coming to life
in real-time,
I tell myself

I love you,

I remind myself

sometimes all you need
is for someone to look at you
and tell you that you're doing the right thing,
that you're not fucking up,
that even after two days without a shower
and your hair unbrushed
and the anxiety from the weekend
still running through your veins,
someone still loves you
more than they did yesterday,
and they will love you more tomorrow
than they did today

and sometimes all you need is reassurance
that someone still cares,

that the person you love
is still there

the little girl inside of me used to scream:

"unloved! unloved! unloved!"

but then I began to tune into her frequency
and give her what she needs

now we hold hands
as I walk her through the park
and tell her all of the things
that I've always loved about her

if love is real
then I know I've found it
in the way that my best friend speaks to me
on my best and worst days,
I know I've found it
in the way that my father hugs me
before he leaves for a business trip
and in the way that my mother
tells me that she still loves me
even after I've had one too many glasses of wine,
I know I've found it
in the way that I wake up every day
to remind myself
that I was put on this planet
to show people
what real love means,
I know I've found it
in the most simple of ways
and that is enough to keep me going,
that is enough
for me to say
that one day
I will have a chance
to share it with another

it has always been enough
to find love
in the most ordinary ways

– if it is about love
it will always be enough

I want to be so full of love
that even a bee sting
feels like a kiss

– I want to be so full of love
that it scares the people around me

to my inner child:

even when you feel as though
you are not deserving of love,
I hope you remember that even then,
I love you more than I've ever loved anyone

– even then,
I still believe you put the stars in the sky

to the one who loves me next:

if you ever need to know anything about me, know this:

I haven't read a romance novel since I was twelve years old;
today I bought one and read the whole thing in one day

if you ever wonder how I fell in love with you, know this:

when I love something
I pour everything I have into it

I couldn't spend one more minute of my life without you in it to my future self:

if I see you around,
I'll tell you all of the stories
about who we were
before I met you

I'll tell you about the boy who broke my heart
and the one who helped pull me out of the dark

I'll show all of my favorite hiding places
and all of the spaces that hold my favorite memories

I'll teach you how to cook my favorite meals
and show you how I like my coffee

I'll be your guiding light
as you put up your best fight
to navigate this crazy thing we call 'life'

I'll always love you
exactly as you are

p.s. I left coffee in the pot for you, too

from my heart to yours, with love

a message from the author

I hope this book reminds you that you deserve to be loved – *kindly and compassionately*. I hope you find the kind of love you want to write about. I hope you find the easy kind of love – the kind of love that doesn't keep you up at night. You deserve the kind of love that fills you up.

I hope you find the person who fills your cup of coffee without you having to ask.

@wordsbycammie

Printed in Great Britain
by Amazon

48466219R00115